WARNING!
THIS BOOK WON'T MAKE
ANYTHING LOOK EASY

You have all read "step-by-step" instruction books that make everything look so easy to do. . .until you try to do it! Well, this book is different. We haven't tried to make anything *look* easy. What we have done is show you *exactly* what to do. . .line by line, fold by fold, cut by cut. . .all spelled out in simple, complete drawings.

So as you flip through this book, don't be surprised at the number of diagrams. You see, we've filled in all the steps those "easy-as-pie," "1-2-3," "do-it-yourself" instruction books leave out.

How To Make
Ties & Tablecloths

by Jerry Kirschen

GROSSET & DUNLAP
A National General Company
Publishers   New York

Printed in the United States of America

CONTENTS

HOW TO READ THIS BOOK

This is not a book to leaf through casually. It's a workbook in the real sense of the word. Choose your first project. . .tie or tablecloth. . .decide on the size of the tie or the shape of the tablecloth that you want and then turn to the correct section. Read each step and look carefully at each drawing. Then, when you've finished reading, buy the materials you'll need and get to work. Once again follow each step. . .but this time work along with the diagrams.

All the directions in this book have been tested by several women who actually followed the directions. . .you'll find them to be clear, exact and easy to understand.

How to Make a Tie

You are about to learn how to design, cut and sew a man's necktie. Since your finished tie will be "hand-made" the instructions will show you how to make a fully lined necktie . . . there'll be none of the manufac-turers' "shortcuts." The necktie you design will be a properly made, handsome gift, something you will be proud to have done.

We are not going to *give* you a pattern from which to work. Instead you will learn how to design your own pattern, step-by-step, for the length and width tie you want to make. First, here's a list of the materials you'll need.

Materials

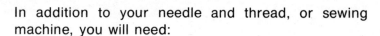

In addition to your needle and thread, or sewing machine, you will need:

1. A yardstick
2. A pair of scissors
3. Tie fabric, 1 yard of 36-inch-wide material
4. Lining fabric, 1 yard of 36-inch-wide material
5. Interfacing, ¼ yard of 36-inch-wide material
6. A pencil
7. Some chalk
8. Paper (brown "Kraft" paper is best—2 sheets, 36 by 14 inches and 28 by 10 inches)

As you know, there are two ends to a tie—the wide end and the narrow end.

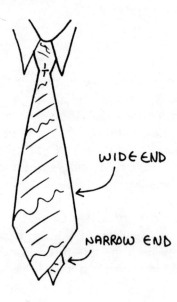

WIDE END

NARROW END

Ties vary in width. Some men like full, wide ties; others like more conservatively proportioned ties. Decide on the width tie *you* want to make (anywhere from 2½ to 5½ inches).

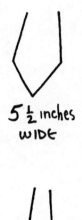

5 ½ inches
WIDE

2 ½ inches
WIDE

Before you start, just to make things clear, let's see how a tie is made. On this finished tie you can see the seam where the wide section is sewn to the narrow section.

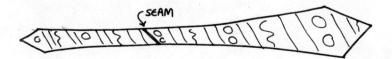

SEAM

Opening the seam separates the tie into its two sections.

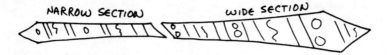

Lifting up the wide end of the tie, you will see another seam.

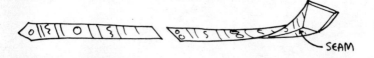

Opening the seam shows how the cloth for the wide section was cut and folded.

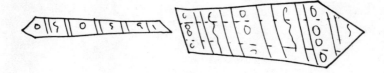

Picking up the narrow section, you will find *its* seam.

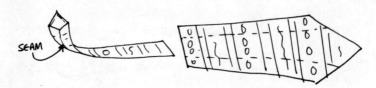

Opening the seam shows how the cloth for the *narrow* end of the tie was cut and folded.

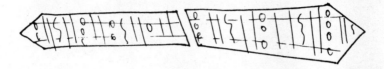

Here are two sample paper patterns, one for the wide section of the tie and another for the narrow section.

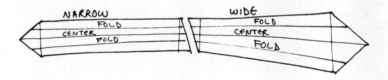

Now let's begin by designing a paper pattern for the wide section of your tie.

Preparing a Pattern

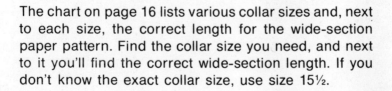

The chart on page 16 lists various collar sizes and, next to each size, the correct length for the wide-section paper pattern. Find the collar size you need, and next to it you'll find the correct wide-section length. If you don't know the exact collar size, use size 15½.

COLLAR SIZE	LENGTH OF WIDE SECTION
13½	30¾ inches
14	31 inches
14½	31¼ inches
15	31½ inches
15½	31¾ inches
16	32 inches
16½	32¼ inches
17	32½ inches
17½	32¾ inches
18	33 inches

Now use your yardstick to draw a line of the proper length (as indicated on the chart). Draw this line across the middle of the larger sheet of paper.

Make a mark exactly 1 inch from the left end of the line.

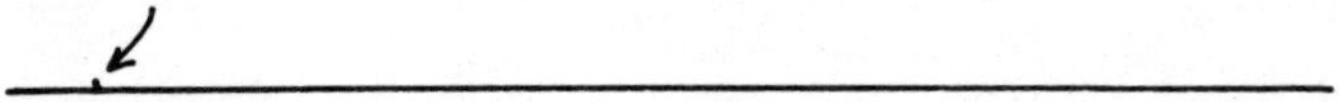

Now make another mark exactly 1 inch to the right of the first mark.

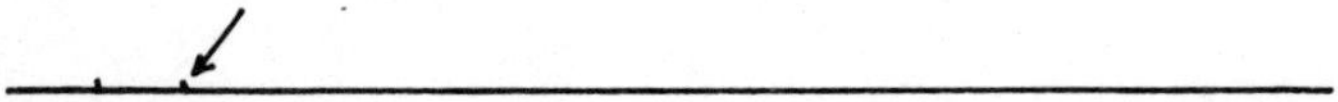

Now draw a line 2 inches long, exactly 1 inch above the line and 1 inch below.

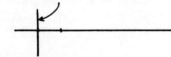

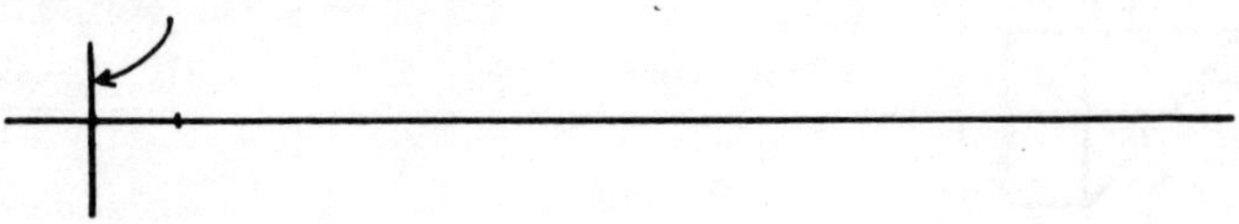

Now draw *this* line . . . 2 inches long, exactly 1 inch above the line and 1 inch below.

Connect the lines as shown.

Draw this line.

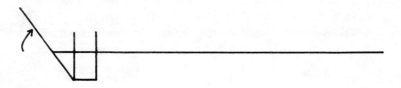

Draw this straight line crossing the first line.

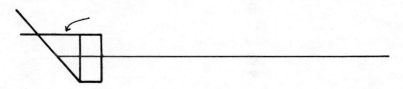

Erase the extra lines so that your drawing looks like this.

You are now to mark another point on the line.

Here's how to determine where to make this mark. Look at the chart below and find the width of tie you wish to make. Next to the chosen width you'll find the correct distance from the right end of the line to mark the point.

WIDTH OF TIE	DISTANCE FROM THE RIGHT END OF THE LINE TO MARK POINT
2½ inches	1½ inches
3 inches	1¾ inches
3½ inches	2 inches
4 inches	2¼ inches
4½ inches	2½ inches
5 inches	2¾ inches
5½ inches	3 inches

Now draw this line through the point you marked.

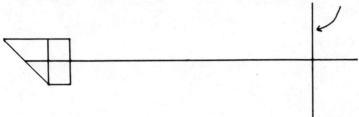

The length of this line will be twice the width of the tie you're designing. If your tie is to be 4 inches wide, the line should go 4 inches above the line and 4 inches below. If your tie is to be 4½ inches wide, the line should go 4½ inches above the line and 4½ inches below the line . . . and so on.

Now draw *this* line.

Draw this line.

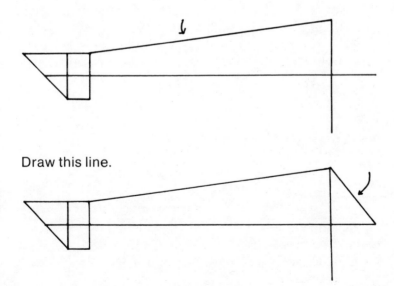

Draw this line.

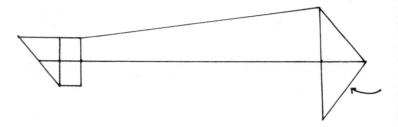

Draw *this* line.

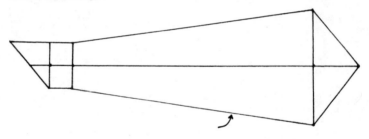

Mark the exact center of this line.

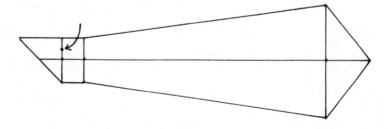

Mark the exact center point of this line.

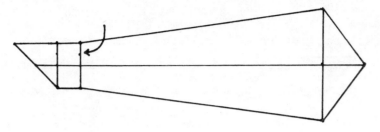

Now mark these four center points.

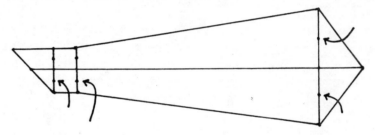

Draw the line shown and write the word "fold" just above the line.

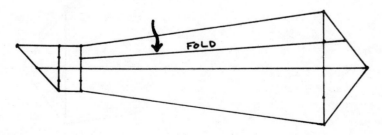

Draw this line.

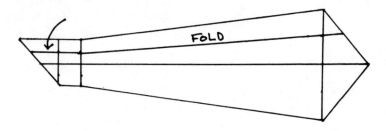

Draw this line.

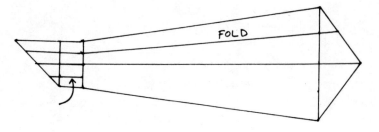

Draw this line and write the word "fold" above the line.

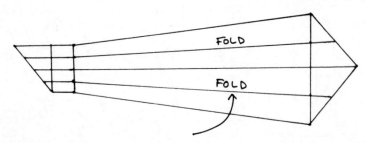

Now write the word "center" over the center line.

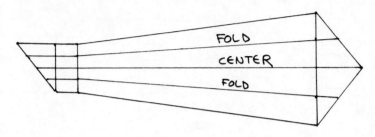

The drawing of the paper pattern is complete except for seam allowances. As you probably know, the seam allowance is an extra bit of cloth to fold under when sewing a seam. In this case the seam allowance will be ⅜ inch.

Draw this line, exactly ⅜ inch away from the top line.

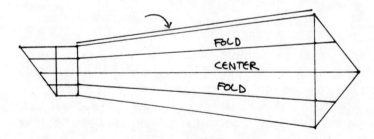

Now draw this line, ⅜ inch away from the tie outline.

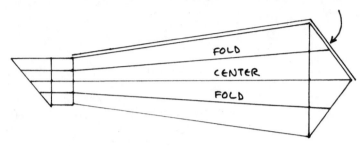

Draw the five remaining lines, each ⅜ inch away from the tie outline.

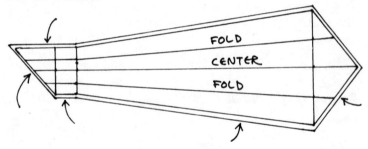

You have now completed designing and drawing the paper pattern for the wide section of your tie. Now carefully cut the pattern out, cutting exactly on the outside, or seam allowance, line. After the pattern is cut out set it aside and begin to work on the paper pattern for the narrow section of the tie.

This chart lists various collar sizes and, next to each size, the correct length for the narrow section. Find the collar size you are working with . . and next to it you'll find the correct narrow-section length. (Remember to use collar size 15½ if you don't know the exact size.)

COLLAR SIZE	LENGTH OF NARROW SECTION
13½	20¾ inches
14	21 inches
14½	21¼ inches
15	21½ inches
15½	21¾ inches
16	22 inches
16½	22¼ inches
17	22½ inches
17½	22¾ inches
18	23 inches

Use your yardstick to draw a line of the proper length.

Mark this point, exactly 1 inch from the right end of the line.

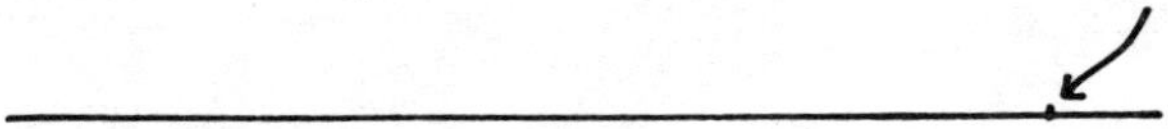

Now mark this point, exactly 1 inch to the left of the first mark.

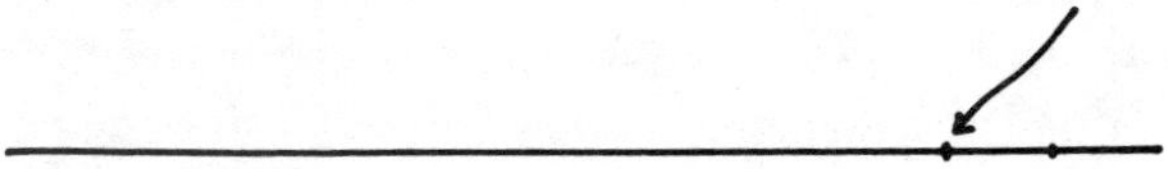

Now draw this line, 2 inches long, exactly 1 inch above the line and 1 inch below.

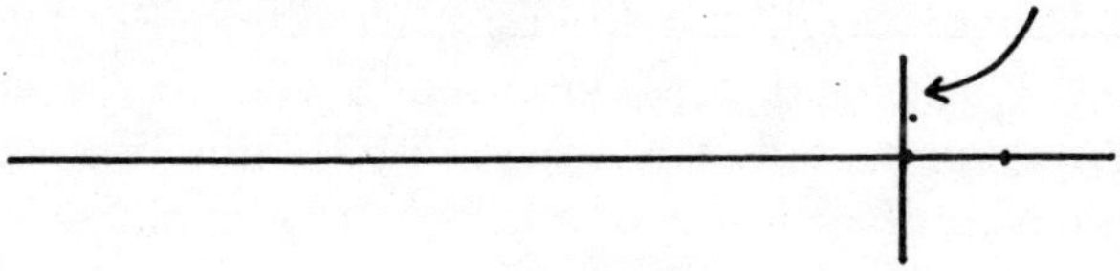

Now draw *this* line . . . 2 inches long, exactly 1 inch above the line and 1 inch below.

Connect the lines as shown.

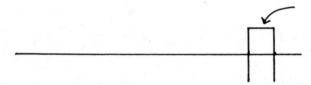

Draw this line.

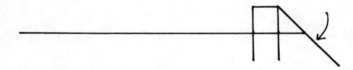

Draw this line.

Erase the extra lines so that your drawing looks like this.

You are now to mark this point on the line.

To do this, look at the chart below and find the width tie you're making. Next to the correct width you'll find the correct distance from the left end of the line to mark the point.

WIDTH OF WIDE END OF TIE	DISTANCE FROM LEFT END OF NARROW SECTION TO MARK POINT
2½ inches	¾ inch
3 inches	¾ inch
3½ inches	¾ inch
4 inches	⅞ inch
4½ inches	1⅛ inches
5 inches	1¼ inches
5½ inches	1¾ inches

You are now going to draw a line through the point you marked. But first look at the chart on page 28. Find the width of the wide section and you'll find next to it the distance above and the distance below to draw the line. For example, if the wide part of the tie is to be 4 inches wide, the line you are now to draw will be 1½ inches above the center line and 1½ inches below. (The total line will be 3 inches long.) If the wide part of the tie is to be 5½ inches wide, the line will extend 3 inches above and 3 inches below for a total of 6 inches.

Now find the width tie you are making and draw the line on your pattern.

WIDTH OF TIE	DISTANCE ABOVE	DISTANCE BELOW	TOTAL LENGTH
2½"	1¼"	1¼"	2½"
3 "	1¼"	1¼"	2½"
3½"	1¼"	1¼"	2½"
4 "	1½"	1½"	3 "
4½"	2 "	2 "	4 "
5 "	2¼"	2¼"	4½"
5½"	3 "	3 "	6 "

Now draw *this* line.

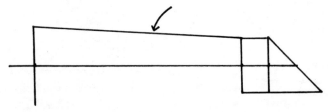

Connect these three lines.

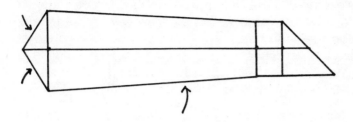

Mark the center of this line.

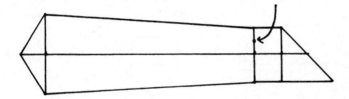

Now mark these five center points.

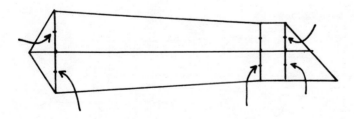

Draw the line shown and write the word "fold" just above the line.

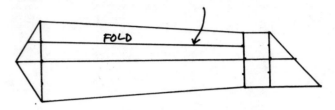

Draw this line.

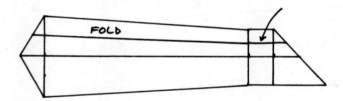

Draw this line.

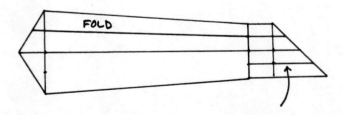

Draw this line and write in the words "fold" and "center."

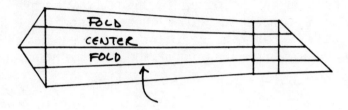

The drawing of the paper pattern is now complete except for the ⅜-inch seam allowance. Draw in these seam allowance lines, each exactly ⅜ inch away from the tie outline.

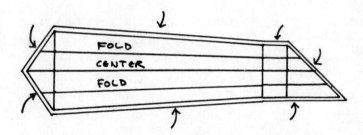

You have now completed the design and drawing of the paper patterns for the narrow section of the tie.

Carefully cut out the pattern, cutting exactly on the outside, or seam allowance, line. After the pattern is cut out you will be ready to use the two patterns you have designed to begin actually cutting the cloth for the tie.

But first a word about tie fabrics and designs.

Fabrics and Designs

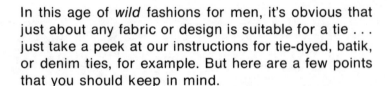

In this age of *wild* fashions for men, it's obvious that just about any fabric or design is suitable for a tie . . . just take a peek at our instructions for tie-dyed, batik, or denim ties, for example. But here are a few points that you should keep in mind.

For your first tie, try to avoid silk or silky materials such as nylon or silky acetates. You may find them a bit difficult to handle.

Don't use very heavy-weight wool or other fabrics. Remember, the tie you will be making will be fully lined, and that means that there will be two thicknesses of lining and two of fabric lying under the shirt collar.

As to designs, as we've pointed out, you can be as wild as you like . . . provided you've got a man to match! A necktie is a very personal gift and a handmade tie is even more so. The pattern of design you choose will be an indication of how well you know your man's taste, so before you buy fabric or decide on a design give some thought to what *his* taste is like.

One last thing . . . you'll be cutting the tie on the "bias." So if you want a tie with diagonal stripes, you have to use a bolt of cloth with vertical or horizontal stripes, and so on.

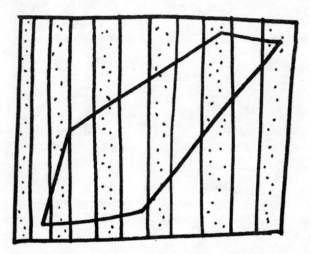

If you are interested in making an embroidered, denim, tie-dyed, appliqué, needlepoint or ink-marked tie, turn to the section called "Something Special." Then turn back and continue following these instructions.

Making the Tie

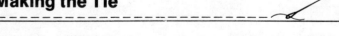

You have designed, drawn and carefully cut out two paper patterns for your tie. Now you will use these two patterns to cut out two fabric "halves," two lining "halves" and two interfacing "halves" to make the tie.

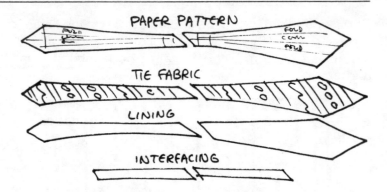

Begin by cutting the two fabric tie "halves." They will be cut to the exact size and shape of the two paper patterns.

If you examine a bolt of cloth closely you will notice that some threads lay lengthwise and some lay widthwise. These threads, woven together, form the cloth itself.

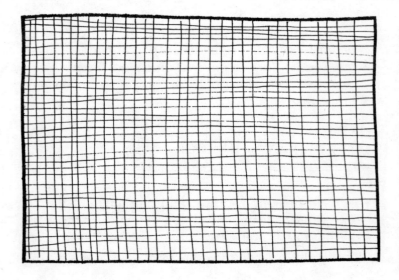

The direction that the threads move in is called the *grain*. There is the lengthwise grain . . .

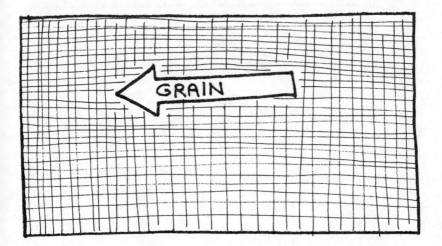

and the widthwise grain.

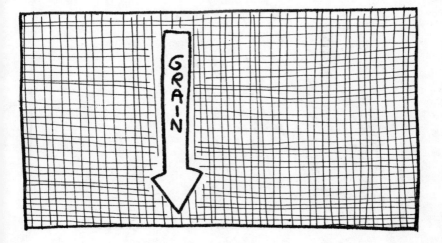

A line exactly halfway between the two grains (on a 45-degree angle to them) is called the bias.

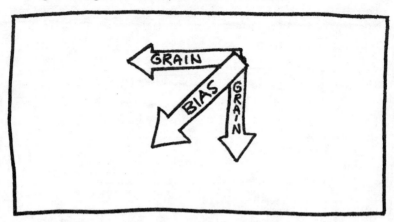

Pin your two paper patterns to the *wrong* side of the fabric so that the center lines of the patterns are "on the bias."

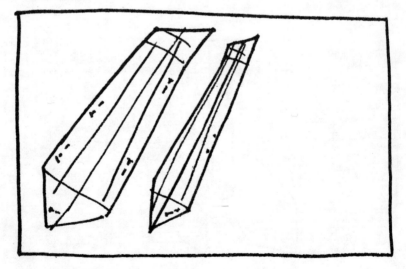

Using a piece of dark chalk for a light fabric or white chalk for a dark fabric, carefully mark the outline of the two paper patterns. Now remove the paper patterns carefully. You'll be using them a few times more. Your fabric should now look something like this.

Carefully cut out the two tie halves. You should now have two fabric tie halves that look something like this.

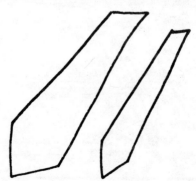

Follow the same steps to trace and cut out the two halves of the tie lining. Use the same paper patterns and cut on the bias. Then, on the "face," or right side, of the lining fabric, chalk in the center line on the lining.

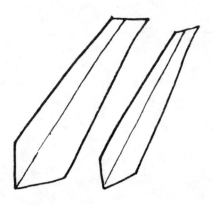

You now have two tie halves, two lining halves and two paper patterns.

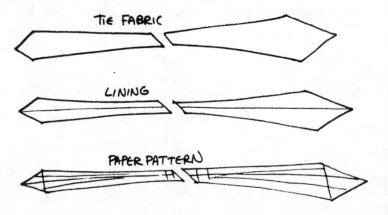

Now you can cut out the interfacing. First cut the two paper patterns along the *fold* lines.

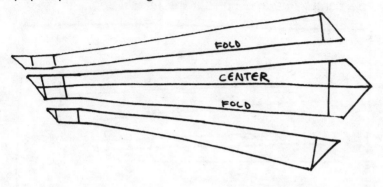

Save the center sections and throw away the side pieces. Cut off the pointed ends of the paper patterns, about 4½ inches from the point of the wide pattern and about 3½ inches from the point of the narrow end.

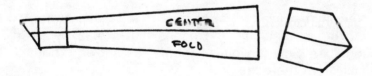

Trim a ¼-inch strip from each side of the paper patterns.

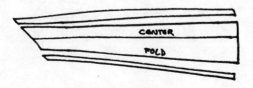

Pin the two patterns to the interfacing material. There's no need to cut on the bias here. Chalk the outlines and the center line and cut out the interfacing.

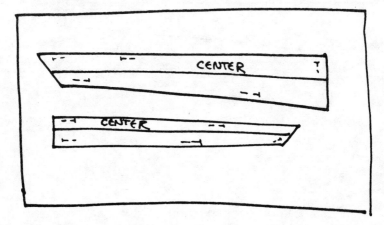

You now have two tie halves, two lining halves and two interfacing halves. At long last you can discard the paper patterns.

Now lay the two tie halves face to face, one on top of the other, matching the edges that are to be sewn together. Sew the ends together as shown (about ⅜ inch from the edge).

Lay the tie face down on the table as shown.

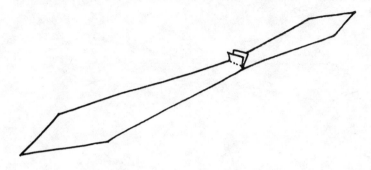

Use an iron to press the seam flat open as shown, then trim the edges of the seam to about ¼ inch.

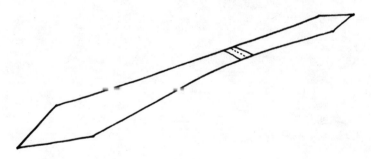

Sew the lining halves together, face to face, just as you did the fabric halves. Then iron the seam flat open and trim to ¼ inch.

Now sew the two halves of the interfacing together. Iron the seam flat open and trim the seam flaps to ¼ inch.

Trim the "points" of the seam flaps on the tie, the lining and the interfacing.

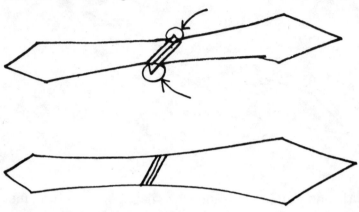

At this point you've got a tie, a tie lining and an interfacing.

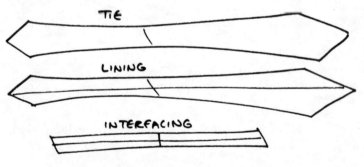

Lay the tie flat on a table, *face up.*

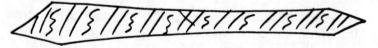

Lay the lining *face down* on top of the tie, and pin it in place. Make sure that all the edges match.

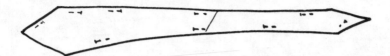

Carefully stitch the lining to the tie, leaving one side open as shown. Remember that the *face* of the lining is being sewn to the *face* of the tie.

The tie, as you have sewn it, is inside out. You must now turn it right side out. But first, trim the seams carefully to ¼ inch.

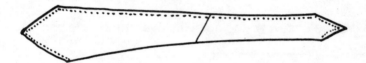

Now turn the tie right side out, using the end of your scissors to push the points of the tie into place.

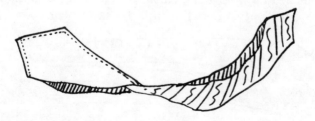

Press the tie flat. Then lay the "lined" tie flat, face down, on a table. You should still be able to see the chalk center line on the lining.

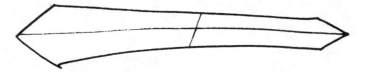

Pin the interfacing to the lining, center line over center line. (The interfacing seam should be right over the lining seam.)

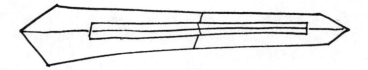

Fold the *unsewn* edge of the tie over the interfacing.

Pin the tie to the interfacing and then sew the edge of the tie to the interfacing, using long running stitches. Take care *not* to sew through the face of the tie.

Remove the pins. Now fold over the second half of the tie and sew it to the first half with a slip stitch.

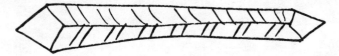

The tie is now completed.

One last word . . . a tie should never be pressed flat. The edges of the tie should be rolls, not sharp creased folds. If your tie needs a pressing, *steam* the tie with a steam iron. Hold the iron just above the tie . . . don't press the iron directly onto the tie!

"Something Special"

In all probability you'll hunt around for an interesting piece of fabric for the tie you'll be making . . . but you just *might* be interested in trying something wild. So here are some interesting and "far-out" tie ideas.

Batik

Batik is a centuries-old process of painting designs on fabric. The word "batik" is Malaysian, and the traditional batik process is still a major industry in parts of Malaysia. This ingenious process has spread throughout the world, and contemporary Western batiks hang in many modern museums and galleries. It is the unique "look" of batik that prompts us to suggest its use in tie design.

For a batik tie you'd do best to use a closely woven, thin cotton fabric. It should be white or a light color, with *no* pattern.

After you've cut out the two tie halves, lay them flat on a newspaper-covered table.

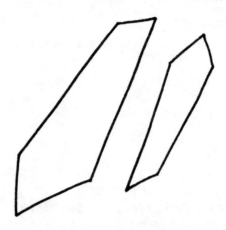

Use a pencil to sketch out a pattern on the tie fabric.

Use a small brush to paint in the design with melted wax. You can pick up the proper wax and batik dyes at most local hobby and craft shops.

When the wax cools and hardens, dunk the tie fabric in a pot of dye. Then stretch out the two tie halves and let them dry. The fabric will be dyed *except* where you painted with wax. In this way you can continue to paint areas of the tie with wax and dunk the fabric into pots of different-colored dyes, allowing the tie to dry between successive waxings. The wax is removed by ironing the material between sheets of absorbent paper so that the wax melts off the fabric and onto the paper. The finished result is a fabric pattern consisting of "overlays" and "washes" of colors . . . the look of batik.

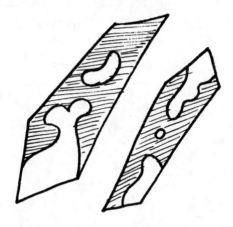

When you've finished the batik work, continue with the regular tie-making instructions.

Tie-Dyeing

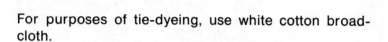

For purposes of tie-dyeing, use white cotton broad-cloth.

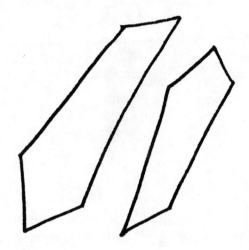

After you've cut out the two tie halves, bunch up some of the material and *tightly* bind it with a rubber band, as shown.

Hold the tie as shown, and dip it into a pot of fabric dye up to the rubber band, *no higher.*

When the tie is opened flat and dry, you'll see the characteristic sunburst pattern of tie-dyeing.

If you wish, you can repeat the process with a second color, bunching up and tying the fabric with a rubber band at a different point.

Repeat these steps with the second half of the tie. When the tie is dry, iron it flat, then continue with the regular tie-making instructions.

Felt Appliqué

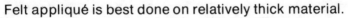

Felt appliqué is best done on relatively thick material.

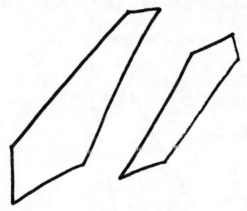

Sketch a few shapes on paper. Make sure that they will fit onto the *face* of the tie (the area between the fold lines). Trace the shapes onto bright-colored felt and cut them out.

Abstract shapes, flowers, birds, fish, fruit, initials or sports equipment such as tennis rackets or golf clubs may be used to design and personalize the tie.

Sew the appliqué to the tie face, using any simple edging stitch. There is no need to fold the felt edges under . . . felt cannot unravel. Make sure to sew the felt designs *between* the fold lines.

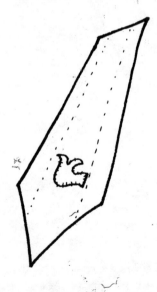

Continue with the regular tie-making procedures.

Denim

After you've cut the tie halves out of denim fabric, lay them on a newspaper-covered work table.

Use an eyedropper or an inexpensive artist's brush to drop, spread or paint swirls of bleach on the denim. Let the denim absorb the bleach a bit . . . then wash the tie halves in cold water.

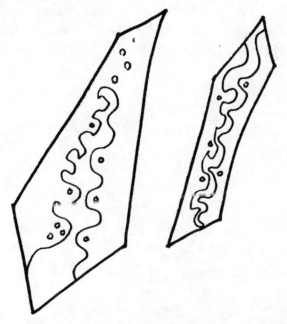

Let dry, then iron the halves flat and continue with the regular instructions. (If you have not worked with bleach before, it is advisable to try out your technique on a scrap or two of denim beforehand. Dilute the bleach if it is too strong.)

Ink Marking

This tie takes a bit of daring.

Use a strong, rather heavy cotton fabric in a solid, light color. After you've cut the tie halves, use several wide felt-tipped markers to "paint" the fabric. Any local art supply store will carry a wide range of bright-colored markers.

Be *bold!* Wide slashes of bright colors can pull it off! Color the whole tie but keep in mind that only the area between the "fold" lines will be the front of the tie.

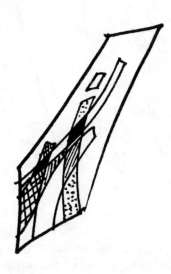

Needlepoint

Here's a new, different and easy way to put your needlepoint to work—a needlepoint tie.

Needlepoint blends best with a tie made of a woolen fabric. After the tie halves are cut out, carefully cut a shape out of the wide end of the tie, making sure that the shape falls well within the *fold* lines. You can cut out any shape ... something abstract, a picture or, as shown here, an initial.

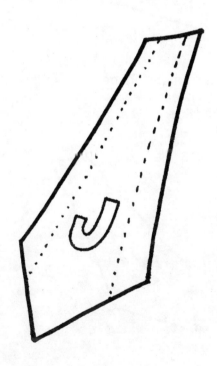

Now sketch a line around the hole you cut. The outline should be exactly 3/16 inch away from the cut edge.

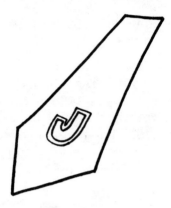

Now cut snips from the shape to the outline, as shown. Be sure to snip each corner and to cut small "V"s around the outside curves.

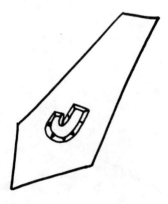

Turn the tie over and press the "flaps" flat back.

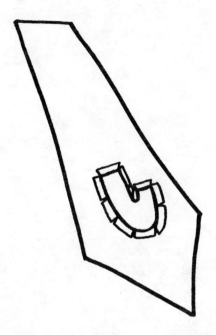

Now do a piece of needlepoint (canvas embroidery) about ¼ inch larger than the shape you cut out of the tie. You can work a pattern or a solid color.

Lay the tie over the embroidery and pin the needlepoint in place.

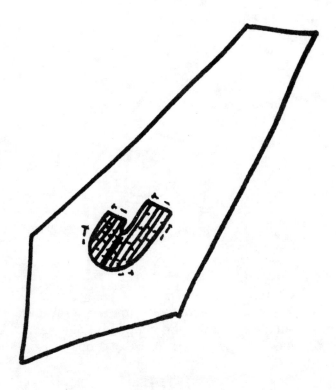

Stitch the tie to the needlepoint, using a blind stitch, hem stitch, slip stitch or any other kind of inconspicuous stitch. Remove the pins and continue with the tie-making instructions.

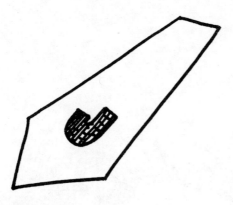

Embroidery

Embroidered ties are a snap! There's just one "trick of the trade" to remember: Do the embroidery on the tie half *after* the tie half has been cut out, but *before* you sew the lining on.

You can, of course, work any kind of embroidery on the tie, but here's a really unusual idea—a paisley-embroidered tie.

Paisley Embroidery

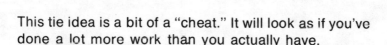

This tie idea is a bit of a "cheat." It will look as if you've done a lot more work than you actually have.

Use a paisley or a paisley-type print for your tie. After the tie halves are cut out, select a needlepoint yarn that matches one of the paisley colors. Try for as close a color match as possible.

Then just sew a simple outline stitch along the paisley outline. Don't follow all the lines—pick one and follow its curls and curves and waves with a easy backstitch. The results are amazing. Now continue with the tie-making instructions.

How to Make a Tablecloth

A Round Cloth

A tablecloth must be wide enough to cover the table and to allow for a "drop" length. On a small, round end-table you might want a floor-length drop, but floor-length is usually a mistake on a dining table.

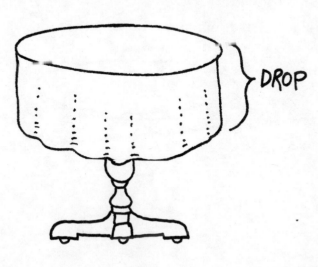

Suppose you have a round table that is 30 inches across and you want a drop of 15 inches. This means that you'll need a round cloth with a diameter of 60 inches.

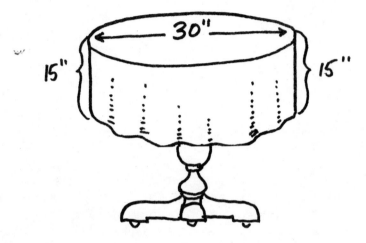

Such a tablecloth is called a "60-inch round."

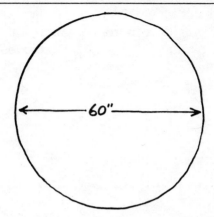

It would be easy to cut a round tablecloth with a diameter of 60 inches ... except for the fact that no standard fabric is made that wide.

Sewing two pieces of cloth together might seem to be a simple solution.

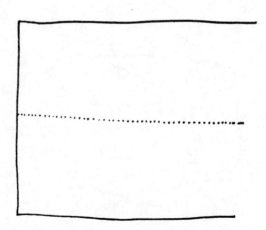

But the result would be a round tablecloth with an unsightly seam across the center.

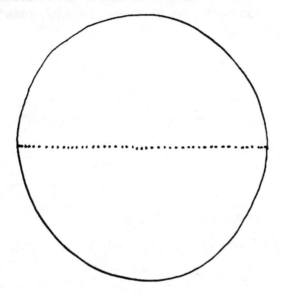

And the cloth would look like this on the table.

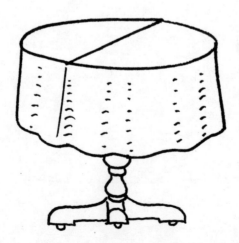

Here's how to make a round tablecloth so that no seam crosses the table top. The tablecloth will have two seams, one on each side . . . neither will cut across the table top.

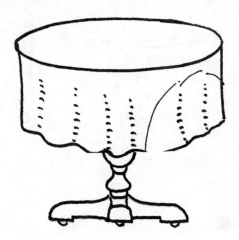

To make the tablecloth, measure the distance from the center of the table to the edge.

Now decide on the length of "drop" that you want.

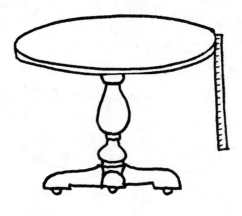

Add the two measurements and write the sum down, adding about 1 inch for a hem. This figure will be the radius of the circle of the tablecloth (half the width of the circle of the tablecloth). Buy a length of fabric *four* times the length of the radius.

Cut the fabric into two equal lengths. You now have two pieces of cloth.

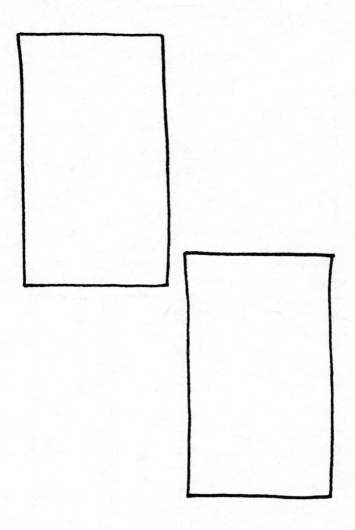

Cut one cloth in half lengthwise. You now have three pieces of cloth.

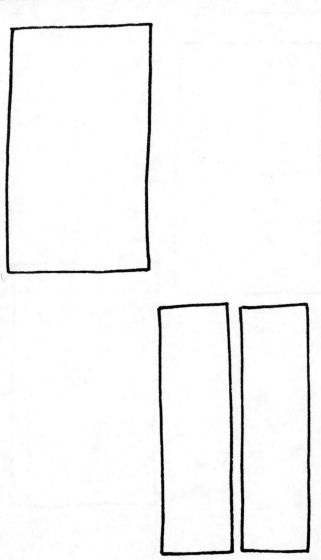

Fold the large piece of cloth in half, as shown.

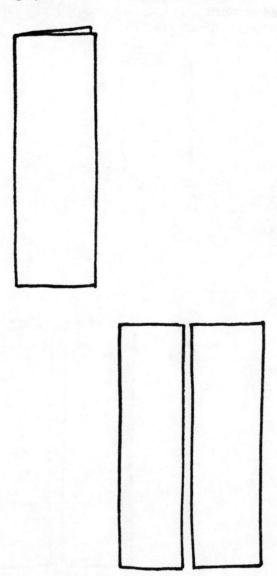

Now fold the cloth in half the other way, and mark the corner shown with chalk or a pin. This is the center point of the piece of cloth.

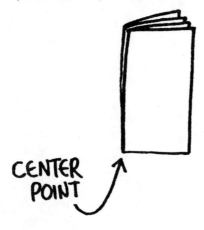

CENTER POINT

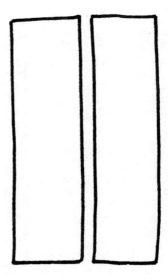

Unfold the cloth. You still have the same three pieces of cloth, but the large piece has the center marked.

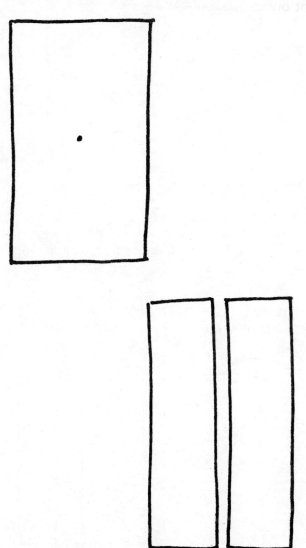

Sew the two smaller pieces to the large piece, as shown. Iron the seams flat and trim to ¼ inch.

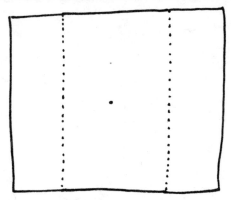

Take a piece of chalk and tie a string to it. The string must be the same length as the radius of the tablecloth. (Remember that the radius is the distance from the center of the table top to the edge, *plus* the drop, *plus* the 1 inch for the hem.)

Hold one end of the string at the center point on the fabric and, with the chalk at the other end, draw a circle.

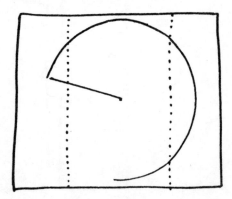

You now have the fabric with two seams, and a chalk circle.

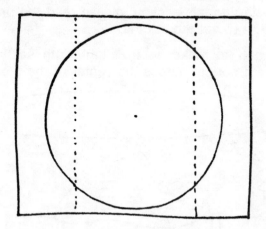

Cut carefully along the chalk circle, and you have your round tablecloth!

Sew the hem, and if desired add decorative trimming to the edge—ball fringe, braid, etc. —and your cloth is done.

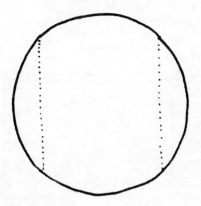

An Oval Cloth

Before starting this section, please read the previous section on round tablecloths.

Here's how to make an oval tablecloth so that the seams will not cut across the center of the table.

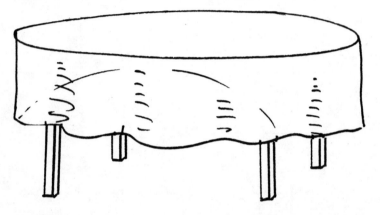

The first step is to find the center of your oval table. Tape a piece of cardboard or paper onto the approximate center of the table.

Measure the length of the table and, on the sheet of paper, draw a straight line to mark the halfway point.

Now measure the width of the table and draw a straight line to measure the exact halfway point. You now have a cross that marks the center of the oval table top.

Take out a blank sheet of paper and draw an oval to represent the oval table top. Draw a cross to represent the center of the oval.

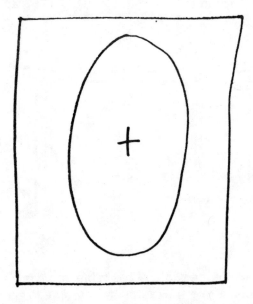

Now measure the distance from the cross to the far edge of the table top.

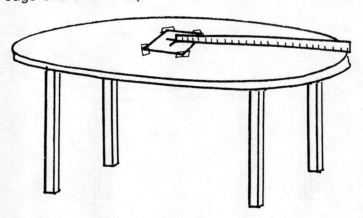

Add the "drop" and 1 inch for the hem. Fill in this figure on your drawing. For example, suppose the distance is 30 inches and you want an 11-inch drop. Add 30 to 11 and add 1 for the hem. The distance will be 42 inches.

Notice that you draw in *two* lines and mark down the distance *twice.*

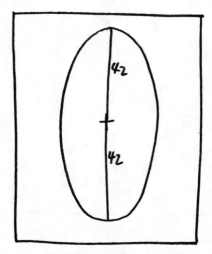

Now measure the distance from the center cross to the "near" edge and add the "drop" and 1 inch for a hem.

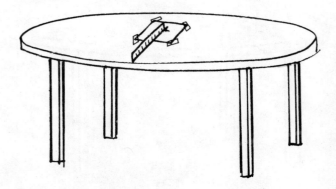

On your drawing, sketch in the lines and draw in the distances, allowing again for the drop and the hem.

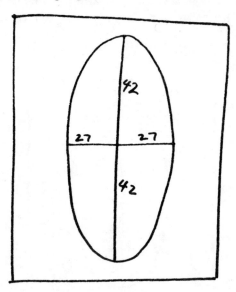

You now have measured the length and the width. Next, measure from the center cross to the edge, halfway between the far and near edge.

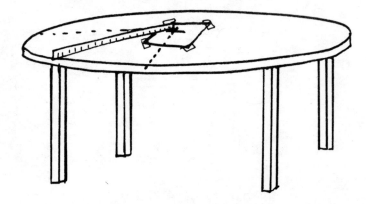

Draw in four lines midway between the lines on your drawing and fill in the distance of each of the four new lines.

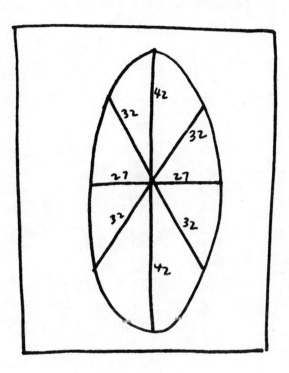

Buy a length of fabric *four* times the length of the longest length indicated on your drawing. (In this example it would be a piece of fabric four times 42 inches, or 168 inches—14 feet.)

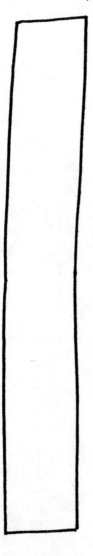

Cut the cloth into two equal pieces as shown.

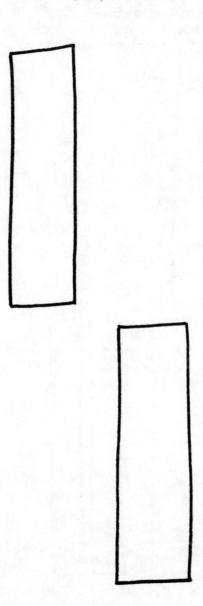

Cut one of the pieces in half.

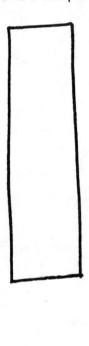

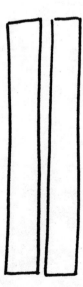

Fold the other piece in half.

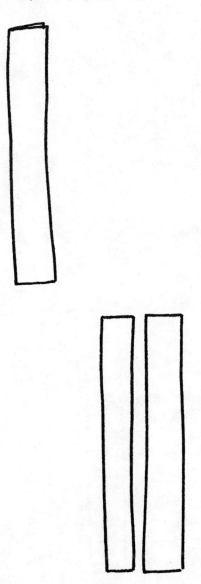

And in half again . . . the corner shown is the center point. Mark it with chalk or a pin.

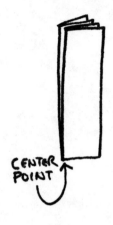

CENTER
POINT

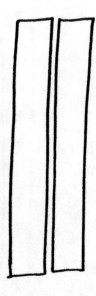

Unfold the cloth. You now have the same three pieces of cloth, but the large piece has the center marked.

Sew the two smaller pieces to the larger piece, as shown.

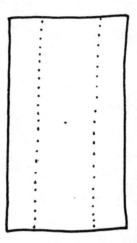

Now use a yardstick and a piece of chalk to mark eight points around the center point. Each point should be marked at the same distance away from the center point as indicated on your sketch.

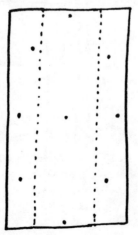

Use a piece of chalk to sketch in the oval, sketching through all eight points.

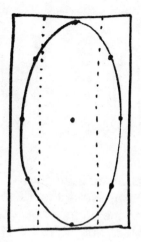

Cut along the chalk oval. Hem, or sew on a decorative binding, and you've got your tailormade oval tablecloth.

Cloths for Oddly Shaped Tables

First read the section on round tablecloths.

Many-sided tables are best covered with round tablecloths. So if you've got a table that is neither round, oval, square or rectangular, follow the directions for the round tablecloth *except:*

1. You're going to have to find the centerpoint of your table top.

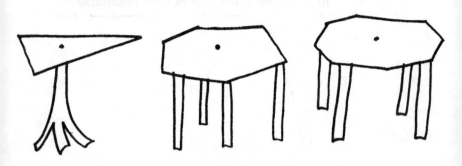

2. When, in the instructions for the round tablecloth, you are asked to "measure the distance from the center of the table to the edge," measure instead from the center of the table to one of the corners of the table.

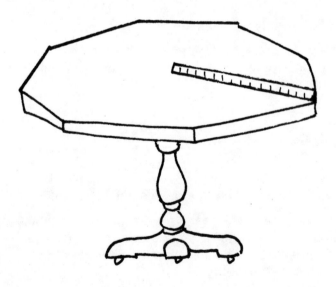

Now turn back to the directions for round tablecloths.

One final note on tablecloths: Except for needlepoint, all of the decorative techniques suggested for ties—batik, tie-dyeing, ink-marking or embroidery—can be used to create interesting and different tablecloths. For example, you can make a tablecloth from a paisley fabric and embroider parts of the design after the cloth is completed. Just follow the directions given for tie design in the section called "Something Special."

About the Author

Jerry Kirschen is both the author and the illustrator of this book. Originally trained as an artist, he later became involved with computers and computer programming and discovered what kind of precise step-by-step directions were necessary to truly simplify complicated procedures. A combining of these painstakingly acquired talents led to a commission by a pattern company to do two sewing books, and now to HOW TO MAKE TIES & TABLECLOTHS.